Cambridge English

OFFICIAL
PREPARATION MATERIAL

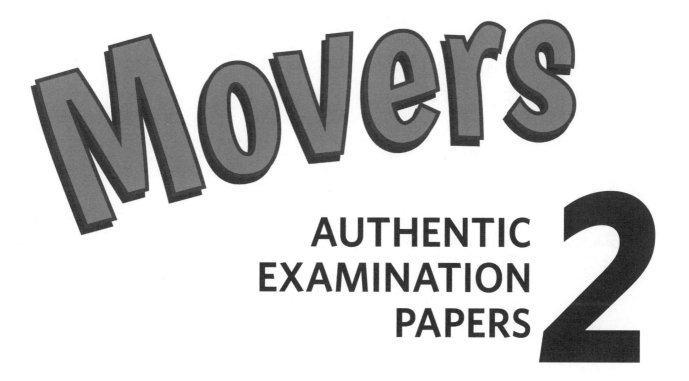

Movers

AUTHENTIC EXAMINATION PAPERS **2**

ANSWER BOOKLET

Cambridge University Press
www.cambridge.org/elt

Cambridge English Language Assessment
www.cambridgeenglish.org

Information on this title: www.cambridge.org/9781316636275

© Cambridge University Press and UCLES 2018

First published 2018

20 19 18 17 16 15 14 13 12 11 10 9 8 7 6 5 4

Printed in Malaysia by Vivar

A catalogue record for this publication is available from the British Library

ISBN 978-1-316-63627-5 Answer Booklet
ISBN 978-1-316-63624-4 Student's Book
ISBN 978-1-316-63630-5 Audio CD

Contents

Introduction

The *Cambridge English: Young Learners* tests offer an elementary-level testing system (up to CEFR level A2) for learners of English between the ages of 7 and 12. The tests include three key levels of assessment: *Starters*, *Movers* and *Flyers*.

Movers is the second level in the system. Test instructions are very simple and consist only of words and structures specified in the syllabus.

The complete test lasts about an hour and has the following components: Listening, Reading and Writing, and Speaking.

	length	number of parts	number of questions
Listening	approx. 25 minutes	5	25
Reading and Writing	30 minutes	6	35
Speaking	5–7 minutes	4	–

Candidates need a pen or pencil for the Reading and Writing paper, and coloured pens or pencils for the Listening paper. All answers are written on the question papers.

Listening

In general, the aim is to focus on the 'here and now' and to use language in meaningful contexts. In addition to multiple-choice and short-answer questions, candidates are asked to use coloured pencils to mark their responses to one task. There are five parts. Each part begins with a clear example.

part	main skill focus	input	expected response	number of items
1	listening for names and descriptions	picture, names and dialogue	draw lines to match names to people in a picture	5
2	listening for names, spellings and other information	form or page of notepad with missing words and dialogue	write words or numbers in gaps	5
3	listening for words, names and detailed information	picture sets and list of illustrated words or names and dialogues	match pictures with illustrated word or name by writing letter in box	5
4	listening for specific information of various kinds	3-option multiple-choice pictures and dialogues	tick boxes under correct pictures	5
5	listening for words, colours and specific information	picture and dialogue	carry out instructions to colour and write (range of colours is: black, blue, brown, green, grey, orange, pink, purple, red, yellow)	5

Reading and Writing

Again, the focus is on the 'here and now' and the use of language in meaningful contexts where possible. To complete the test, candidates need a single pen or pencil. There are six parts, each starting with a clear example.

part	main skill focus	input	expected response	number of items
1	reading short definitions and matching to words writing words	labelled pictures and definitions	copy the correct words next to definitions	5
2	reading a dialogue and choosing the correct responses	short dialogue with multiple-choice responses	choose correct response by circling a letter	6
3	reading for specific information and gist copying words	gapped text, labelled pictures and one 3-option multiple choice	choose and copy missing words correctly; tick a box to choose the best title for the story	6
4	reading and understanding a factual text copying words	gapped text and 3-option multiple choice	complete text by selecting the correct words and copying them in corresponding gaps	5
5	reading a story completing sentences	story, pictures and gapped sentences	complete sentences about story by writing 1, 2 or 3 words	7
6	completing sentences, responding to questions and writing sentences about a picture	picture, sentence prompts and questions	complete sentences, answer questions and write full sentences	6

Speaking

In the Speaking test, the candidate speaks with one examiner for about six minutes. The format of the test is explained in advance to the child in their native language, by a teacher or person familiar to them. This person then takes the child into the exam room and introduces them to the examiner.

Speaking ability is assessed according to various criteria, including comprehension, the ability to produce an appropriate response and pronunciation.

part	main skill focus	input	expected response
1	describing two pictures by using short responses	two similar pictures	identify four differences between pictures
2	understanding the beginning of a story and then continuing it based on a series of pictures	picture sequence	describe each picture in turn
3	suggesting a picture which is different and explaining why	picture sets	identify the odd one out and give reason
4	understanding and responding to personal questions	open-ended questions about candidate	answer personal questions

Further information

Further information about *Cambridge English: Young Learners* can be obtained from:

Cambridge English Language Assessment   www.cambridgeenglish.org/help
1 Hills Road   www.cambridgeenglish.org/younglearners
Cambridge CB1 2EU
United Kingdom

Test 1 Answers

Listening

Part 1 (5 marks)

Lines should be drawn between:

1 Clare and the girl feeding the sheep
2 Jack and the boy walking up the field, near the cows
3 Peter and the man building the wall
4 Zoe and the girl riding on the horse
5 Julia and the woman carrying vegetables, behind the tractor

Part 2 (5 marks)

1 Gate   2 Friday(s)   3 98/ninety-eight
4 weather   5 (a) rainbow

Part 3 (5 marks)

1 shopping centre – G (water plants)
2 cinema – A (milkshake)
3 park – F (listening to radio)
4 station – B (cake)
5 sports centre – D (ice skating)

Part 4 (5 marks)

1 C   2 B   3 A   4 B   5 B

Part 5 (5 marks)

1 Colour the top of the round table – blue (NOT the table legs)
2 Colour the star on the floor – yellow
3 Write SALAD under the words 'Choose a'
4 Colour the cup carried by the woman on a tray – orange (NOT the man's cup)
5 Colour the scarf on the customer by the door – purple

TRANSCRIPT   *Hello. This is the Cambridge English Movers Listening Test.*

Part 1   *Look at Part 1. Now look at the picture. Listen and look. There is one example.*

BOY: Here's a picture of the farm that we went to on our school trip, Mum.
WOMAN: It's great! Who's that person? The man who's coming out of the field?
BOY: With the water? That's Paul. He's the farmer's son.
WOMAN: Oh! He looks busy!
BOY: He was!

Can you see the line? This is an example. Now you listen and draw lines.

1

WOMAN: Is that one of your classmates? The child that's with the sheep?
BOY: Yes. Her name's Clare. She's feeding them.
WOMAN: That's nice. They're very young.
BOY: Yes. They were only six weeks old, I think.

2

BOY: And there's Jack. He's walking up the top field to see the cows. Look!
WOMAN: Oh yes. Was he afraid of them? Cows are huge animals!
BOY: Well, he took a photo of them with his tablet and then came back down again very quickly!
WOMAN: OK!

3

BOY: And I talked to that person. He knew a lot. He helps on the farm.

WOMAN: Do you mean the man who's building that wall?

BOY: Yes. He's called Peter.

WOMAN: Oh!

BOY: He often has to fix the walls. They fall down a lot.

4

WOMAN: Who's that? On the horse?

BOY: Let me think ... Oh, I know. That's Zoe. It was her first riding lesson.

WOMAN: Did she enjoy it?

BOY: Yes. I'd like to try that one day, too.

WOMAN: Me too.

5

BOY: And can you see the woman who's carrying the vegetables?

WOMAN: No, where is she?

BOY: Behind the tractor. She's called Julia.

WOMAN: Oh yes! How do you know her name?

BOY: She talked to us about growing different things. She was really nice. We had a great day there.

WOMAN: Good!

Now listen to Part 1 again.

[The recording is repeated.]

That is the end of Part 1.

Part 2   *Listen and look. There is one example.*

MAN: Which teacher gave you that book, Vicky?

GIRL: He's called Mr Story.

MAN: Mr Story! It's a great name for a teacher, I think!

GIRL: Yes, it is.

Can you see the answer? Now you listen and write.

1

GIRL: It's my new English book, Dad.

MAN: What's it called, Vicky?

GIRL: It's called 'The Gate'. You spell that G-A-T-E. It's fantastic.

MAN: Oh, 'The Gate'! That's a good name!

2

MAN: Is this for your favourite lesson on Fridays?

GIRL: Yes. The lesson on Friday is always the best.

MAN: Why?

GIRL: Because we talk a lot!

MAN: Oh ... *(laughs)*

3

MAN: How many pages are there in your book?

GIRL: Lots. There are 98. Look.

MAN: Wow, 98!

GIRL: But on the last 10 pages, there are only songs.

4

MAN: Well, what's the first part of the book about?

GIRL: The weather!

MAN: Isn't it boring to read about that?

GIRL: No! I like learning about the weather because it's different in different countries!

MAN: Oh! OK!

5

MAN: And have you got to do some homework today?

GIRL: Yes, I've got to write about a picture in the book.

MAN: Which picture? This one of the mountains?

GIRL: Not that one. This one. Look. It's a rainbow.

MAN: A rainbow! Wow! It's beautiful!

Now listen to Part 2 again.

[The recording is repeated.]

That is the end of Part 2.

Part 3   *Listen and look. There is one example.*

Grandpa is telling Jim about different places he goes to. What does Grandpa enjoy doing in these places?

BOY: Hello, Grandpa. How are you and how's your new flat?

MAN: I'm fine, thank you, Jim. I enjoy living here a lot.

BOY: Good.

MAN: I go to the library every day after lunch and look at the maps there. I love doing that.

Can you see the letter E? Now you listen and write a letter in each box.

1

MAN: I go to the shopping centre every day too. I like helping a man who works there.

BOY: How do you help him?

MAN: I water the plants when I'm there. It's fun!

BOY: Are there a lot of plants?

MAN: Yes, there are.

2

BOY:	What about the cinema? Do you like going there, too?
MAN:	Yes, but not to watch films!
BOY:	What, then?
MAN:	I stop there to have a milkshake! They make the best ones in town there!
BOY:	Wow!

3

MAN:	The park in the town centre is really good.
BOY:	Right!
MAN:	I sit there between eleven and twelve o'clock every day ... and listen to the radio on my phone.
BOY:	Do you?
MAN:	Yes. There's always something good to listen to then. I like being there because it's beautiful.

4

BOY:	And is your new flat near the station?
MAN:	It's not very near, but I enjoy walking there most days.
BOY:	Why do you do that?
MAN:	There's a great café there with the best cakes in town!

5

MAN:	Oh! And there's a brilliant sports centre here, Jim.
BOY:	That's good!
MAN:	The pool's very big, but I don't go swimming there.
BOY:	What do you do there, then?
MAN:	Ice skating. I really enjoy that!
BOY:	*(laughs)* That's fantastic, Grandpa!
MAN:	Yes, I know.

Now listen to Part 3 again.

[The recording is repeated.]

That is the end of Part 3.

Part 4 *Look at the pictures. Listen and look. There is one example.*

What can Daisy do now?

GIRL:	Can we make pizzas now, Dad?
MAN:	Not today, Daisy. I'm too busy, sorry. Why don't you do some piano practice?
GIRL:	I can't do that, Dad. I haven't got my music book here.
MAN:	OK. Well, are you enjoying your new e-book?
GIRL:	Yes, it's great. I can read some more of that!

Can you see the tick? Now you listen and tick the box.

1 Where is Lily?

WOMAN:	Where's Lily? Do you know?
BOY:	She went for a walk by the waterfall, I think, Mum.
WOMAN:	Oh! Here's a text from her. She's in the village.
BOY:	Who's she with?
WOMAN:	Her new friend who lives near the forest.

2 Which is Charlie's dad?

WOMAN:	What does your father do, Charlie? Is he a teacher like me?
BOY:	No, he's a train driver!
WOMAN:	Wow. What exciting work! I wanted to be a clown when I was young!
BOY:	Really? *(laughs)*

3 What did Sally see?

MAN:	Can you bring that garden chair inside please, Sally?
GIRL:	OK. Oh! What's that? Under one of the chair legs. Is it a sweet?
MAN:	Where? Oh ... It's a little leaf, I think ...
GIRL:	No, it's not. It's a snail, Dad.

4 Who does Nick want to phone?

WOMAN:	Who are you phoning, Nick? Your school friend Mary again?
BOY:	That's right. I want to tell her about Aunt Jane's website.
WOMAN:	Oh ... Can you do that after dinner? Your big brother's here! He's back from his holiday!
BOY:	Great! OK.

5 What is the matter with Eva?

MAN:	What's the matter, Eva? Have you got a stomach-ache?
GIRL:	No, Dad. My tooth's hurting again. That's all.
MAN:	Well, would you like something to drink?
GIRL:	No, thanks. Please don't worry and don't tell Mum. She's got a headache.

Now listen to Part 4 again.

[The recording is repeated.]

That is the end of Part 4.

Part 5 *Look at the picture. Listen and look. There is one example.*

WOMAN:	Would you like to colour some of this café picture now?
BOY:	Yes, please!
WOMAN:	Good. Well, there's a coffee machine. Can you see it?
BOY:	Yes! Can I colour that brown?
WOMAN:	All right!

Can you see the brown coffee machine? This is an example. Now you listen and colour and write.

1

WOMAN: Now colour the round table, but only the top.
BOY: OK. Can I choose the colour?
WOMAN: Yes, you can.
BOY: Then I'd like to colour that blue, please. I've got that colour here.
WOMAN: Fine!

2

BOY: What now?
WOMAN: You can colour a star ... the one on the floor.
BOY: Right. How about green for that?
WOMAN: No, let's make that yellow.
BOY: OK. That's a nice colour, too ...

3

WOMAN: We need to write something here, too. Can you see the square board?
BOY: The one that says 'Choose a ...' on it?
WOMAN: Yes. Write SALAD under those words, please.
BOY: OK. We often eat that at home!
WOMAN: So do we!

4

WOMAN: I'd like you to colour a cup now.
BOY: All right. Can I colour the cup that the woman's carrying?
WOMAN: Yes, please. Make it orange.
BOY: Oh ... I love that colour. The man's got a cup, too.
WOMAN: Yes, I know. But don't colour that one.

5

BOY: And can I colour someone's scarf?
WOMAN: Yes. Colour the one that the person at the door is wearing.
BOY: Cool. Purple?
WOMAN: Yes! Good idea!
BOY: Great. There!
WOMAN: Very good! Thank you for all your colouring. The picture looks fantastic now.

Now listen to Part 5 again.

[The recording is repeated.]

That is the end of the Movers Listening Test.

Reading and Writing

Part 1 (5 marks)

1 a film star   2 mountains   3 a picnic
4 a doctor   5 a forest

Part 2 (6 marks)

1 C   2 A   3 B   4 C   5 A   6 B

Part 3 (6 marks)

1 grass   2 run   3 parents   4 hungry
5 pie   6 Dan and the pear tree

Part 4 (5 marks)

1 sometimes   2 of   3 these
4 wait   5 their

Part 5 (7 marks)

1 shopping/driving   2 (small/little) car
3 milk and eggs   4 (good) website
5 sunny (holiday) places   6 homework   7 help

Part 6 (10 marks)

Questions 1 and 2 have a maximum score of 1 mark each. Questions 3–6 have a maximum score of 2 marks each. Please see the Cambridge English: Young Learners 2018 Handbook for Teachers *for further details of how marks are awarded.*

Possible answers:

1 playing (with a dog)/looking at/smiling at a dog
2 (red) door
3 a (pink) jacket/(yellow) boots/a (pink) hat/a (purple) skirt/a (yellow) T-shirt
4 sandwiches/drinks/salad/(orange/apple) juice/tea, etc
5 There is a bag next to the seat.
6 A woman has got a small dog.

Speaking

Part	Examiner does this:	Examiner says this:	Minimum response expected from child:	Back-up questions:
	Usher brings in and introduces candidate to examiner.			
	Candidate enters.	Hello. My name's *Jane/ Ms Smith*.	Hello.	
		How old are you, *?	*ten*	Are you *ten*?
1	Points to **Find the Differences** pictures.	**Look at these pictures. They look the same, but some things are different.**		
		Here there are two cows, but here there are three cows.		
		What other different things can you see?	Describes four other differences:	Point to other differences the candidate does not mention.
			• yellow/red bus	Give first half of response:
			• man standing/sitting under tree	
			• book/scarf	**Here the bus is yellow, but here …**
			• cloudy/sunny day	
2	Points to **Picture Story**. Allows time to look at the pictures.	**These pictures show a story. It's called 'Clare's birthday'. Look at the pictures first.**		
		It's Clare's birthday today. She's coming home from school. She's thinking about all her presents.		
		Now you tell the story. (pointing at the other pictures)	(Many variations possible)	Point at the pictures. Ask questions about the pictures.
			Clare's at home now. There aren't any presents. She's sad.	**Where is Clare now? Are there any presents?**
			All Clare's friends are in the living room. Clare's very surprised.	**Who's in the living room? Is Clare surprised?**
			Clare's with her friends. She's got lots of presents. She's very happy.	**What are Clare and her friends doing? Has she got lots of presents? Is she happy?**

* Remember to use the child's name throughout the test.

Part	Examiner does this:	Examiner says this:	Minimum response expected from child:	Back-up questions:
3	Shows candidate **Odd-one-out** pictures. Reveals, using separate blank card, each set of pictures in turn.	**Now look at these four pictures.** **One is different. The book is different.** **A lemon, a pineapple and an orange are fruit. You eat them. You don't eat a book. You read it.** **Now you tell me about these pictures. Which one is different? (Why?)**	Candidate suggests a difference (any plausible difference is acceptable).	**What colour are these animals?** (brown) **And this?** (black) **What are these people doing?** (washing) **And this girl?** (sitting) **Where are these people?** (inside) **And this boy?** (outside)
4	Puts away all pictures.	**Now let's talk about hobbies and sports.** **When do you play computer games?** **What do you like reading?** **Where do you watch television?** **Tell me about your favourite sport.**	*after school* *comics* *(in the) living room* *I like football. I play with my friends.*	**Do you play computer games after school?** **Do you like reading comics?** **Do you watch television in the living room?** **What sport do you like? Who do you play with?**
		OK, thank you, *. Goodbye.	Goodbye.	

* Remember to use the child's name throughout the test.

Test 2 Answers

Listening

Part 1 (5 marks)
Lines should be drawn between:
1 Charlie and the boy in the blue jacket, ice skating
2 Zoe and the girl in the yellow hat, on the mountain
3 Jim and the boy eating noodles
4 Paul and the boy making a snowman
5 Clare and the girl with a hot drink

Part 2 (5 marks)
1 Eagle   2 (some) donkeys/donkey   3 catch
4 pancakes/pancake   5 Grace

Part 3 (5 marks)
1 forest – H (feeding horses)
2 swimming pool – A (milkshakes)
3 city centre – F (roller skating)
4 circus – D (listening to band)
5 farm – G (watching TV)

Part 4 (5 marks)
1 C   2 A   3 B   4 A   5 C

Part 5 (5 marks)
1 Colour the smaller pirate's coat – blue
2 Colour the girl's swimsuit – purple
3 Write WAVES after 'big' on the sign
4 Colour the snail in the net – green
5 Colour the big box next to the girl – pink

TRANSCRIPT   *Hello. This is the Cambridge English Movers Listening Test.*

Part 1   *Look at Part 1. Now look at the picture. Listen and look. There is one example.*

GIRL: Look, Mr Parrot. Here's a photo of my friends in the snow!
MAN: It's a fantastic picture!
GIRL: Yes. Look – there's my sister, Julia.
MAN: She's taking a photo.
GIRL: Yes, of the penguin! It was very funny.

Can you see the line? This is an example. Now you listen and draw lines.

1

MAN: Who's that?
GIRL: Do you mean the boy on the ice? That's my friend Charlie.
MAN: He's skating. Is he good at that?

GIRL: No, he isn't! He falls a lot.
MAN: So do I.

2

GIRL: Can you see the girl in the yellow hat?
MAN: Which one? The one on the mountain?
GIRL: Yes. That's Zoe. She's my sister.
MAN: She's going very quickly!
GIRL: I know. She's really brave.

3

MAN: Who's that boy?
GIRL: Oh, you mean Jim? He's my brother's best friend.
MAN: Oh, is he? That's good. What's he eating?
GIRL: He's got some noodles because he's always hungry!
MAN: Mm! I love those!

4

GIRL: Look! Can you see the boy who's sitting in the snow?
MAN: Yes, who's he?
GIRL: He's called Paul.
MAN: He's making a man out of snow.
GIRL: Yes! It's brilliant!

5

MAN: And is that Clare? The girl with a hot drink?
GIRL: Yes. She's drinking some hot chocolate.
MAN: That's nice in this weather.
GIRL: Yes, it is.
MAN: They're all having fun. It's a great picture.
GIRL: Thanks!

Now listen to Part 1 again.

[The recording is repeated.]

That is the end of Part 1.

Part 2 *Listen and look. There is one example.*

MAN: What did you do at the weekend, Sally?
GIRL: I went to the funfair with my family. It was fantastic!
MAN: Oh, great. Did you go on Saturday?
GIRL: Yes, we went on Saturday afternoon.

Can you see the answer? Now you listen and write.

1

MAN: Did you go on any rides at the funfair?
GIRL: Oh, yes! We went on lots of them!
MAN: Which was your favourite?
GIRL: It was called 'Eagle'.
MAN: How do you spell 'Eagle'?
GIRL: It's E-A-G-L-E. It was the best!

2

GIRL: We saw some animals at the funfair, too.
MAN: Oh, did you? What did you see?
GIRL: There was a big field there and we saw some donkeys.
MAN: Donkeys! Wow!
GIRL: Little children could sit on them. It was great.

3

MAN: Were there any games to play at the funfair?
GIRL: Yes. We played a game called 'catch the fish'!
MAN: Catch the fish? Really?
GIRL: It's OK. They were toy fish! We had to close our eyes and find them in the water.
MAN: (*laughs*) That's fun!

4

GIRL: We had some food at the funfair, too.
MAN: Did you? Did you have fries? I know you love those.

GIRL: No, we didn't. We had pancakes!
MAN: Mm, were they good?
GIRL: The pancakes were amazing!

5

MAN: Did you see any friends of yours at the funfair?
GIRL: Yes, I saw one of my best friends there.
MAN: You mean Kim? She loves funfairs!
GIRL: No, it was Grace.
MAN: Oh. Did Grace enjoy it?
GIRL: Yes, she said it was fantastic!

Now listen to Part 2 again.

[The recording is repeated.]

That is the end of Part 2

Part 3 *Listen and look. There is one example.*

Jack and Jane are friends. They do lots of things at the weekends. What did they do in these places?

WOMAN: What did you do at the weekend, Jack?
BOY: Lots of things! On Saturday morning I went to the market with Jane.
WOMAN: Oh, did you? Did you enjoy it?
BOY: Yes, we did. We walked around and looked at lots of things. We bought some nice kiwis.
WOMAN: Great.

Can you see the letter C? Now you listen and write a letter in each box.

1

BOY: On Saturday afternoon we went to the forest.
WOMAN: Oh, I like it there. There are some really old trees.
BOY: Yes, there are. And did you know that there are horses there?
WOMAN: No, I didn't! Are there many of them?
BOY: Yes – and we fed them!
WOMAN: Oh, I didn't know you could do that.

2

WOMAN: Did you do something on Saturday morning?
BOY: Yes, we did. We went to the swimming pool.
WOMAN: Did you enjoy that?
BOY: It was good, but we were very thirsty after that and we had a milkshake.
WOMAN: That's nice.
BOY: Yes, you can buy very good ones there.

3

WOMAN: What did you do on Sunday?
BOY: We went into the city centre.

WOMAN: I love going shopping there. Did you do that?

BOY: No, I don't like that. We went roller skating!

WOMAN: Did you? That's good.

4

BOY: We went to a circus on the Sunday afternoon.

WOMAN: Oh, great! What did you see there?

BOY: Well, there was a band. They played some brilliant music and we loved listening to them.

WOMAN: Great!

5

WOMAN: What did you do on Sunday evening?

BOY: We went to my uncle's farm in the countryside.

WOMAN: Oh, did you ride there on your bikes?

BOY: No, we walked there. We were tired. So then we watched a film on TV all evening.

WOMAN: Oh. Was it good?

BOY: It was OK.

WOMAN: Well, you had a very busy weekend!

Now listen to Part 3 again.

[The recording is repeated.]

That is the end of Part 3.

Part 4 *Look at the pictures. Listen and look. There is one example.*

What is Vicky's brother's work?

MAN: What does your brother do, Vicky? Is he a soccer player?

GIRL: That's his hobby, but he doesn't do that for work. He's a farmer.

MAN: Oh, I see. And what about you? What do you want to do?

GIRL: I want to be a movie star!

MAN: (laughs)

Can you see the tick? Now you listen and tick the box.

1 What does Fred want to eat?

WOMAN: Do you want some lunch now, Fred?

BOY: Yes, please, Mum, but not salad. I'd like cheese sandwiches again.

WOMAN: We had those yesterday. Let's have some nice tomato soup.

BOY: No, I don't want that, Mum.

WOMAN: Oh, Fred!

2 Where is the cat?

BOY: Where's the cat, Mary?

GIRL: I don't know. Is she sleeping on your bed again?

BOY: No. She isn't there. Sometimes she sits on the sofa but she isn't there now.

GIRL: Look! There she is. She's asleep on top of Mum's laptop!

BOY: (laughs) That's funny!

3 What is Lily doing now?

WOMAN: What's Lily doing? She's making a lot of noise upstairs! Is she practising her singing?

BOY: No, she isn't. She's reading her book.

WOMAN: But why is she so loud?

BOY: Lily isn't making any noise. Dad's listening to the radio.

4 What did Peter do today?

MAN: Did you have a good day at school, Peter?

BOY: Yes, Dad. I scored a goal when we played hockey!

MAN: Well done! And what's this?

BOY: It's my model tractor. We made them yesterday.

MAN: It's great! And is this your book about the moon and the stars?

BOY: Yes. I've got to read it for Friday. I can start tomorrow.

5 What is the weather like today?

GIRL: It's my birthday party today, Dad! Let's look at the weather. Oh, no!

MAN: What's the matter, Daisy?

GIRL: It's cloudy, Dad! I want to have my birthday party in the garden.

MAN: Well, we can. It isn't raining.

GIRL: But it's windy, too!

MAN: That's OK. It isn't cold outside.

Now listen to Part 4 again.

[The recording is repeated.]

That is the end of Part 4.

Part 5 *Look at the picture. Listen and look. There is one example.*

WOMAN: Do you like this picture?

BOY: Yes, I do! It's great! Can I colour something?

WOMAN: Yes. How about colouring the ball on the beach?

BOY: OK. Can I do it orange?

WOMAN: Yes, that's a good colour.

Can you see the orange ball? This is an example. Now you listen and colour and write.

1

BOY: I can see two pirates in the picture.

WOMAN: Yes, they're in the boat.

BOY: Shall I colour one of them?

WOMAN: Well, colour the smaller one's coat.

BOY: What colour shall I do it?

WOMAN: How about blue?

BOY: OK.

14

2

WOMAN:	Can you see the girl in the picture?
BOY:	Yes, I can. She's sitting on her towel.
WOMAN:	That's right. She's got a new swimsuit, I think!
BOY:	Yes, it's very nice. Can I colour that?
WOMAN:	Yes. Make it purple.
BOY:	Cool! I like that colour.

3

BOY:	I don't think they can go swimming today.
WOMAN:	No, it's dangerous! Can you see where it says that?
BOY:	Yes, I can.
WOMAN:	Write WAVES after 'big'.
BOY:	Mmm, you can't swim when there are very big waves. OK, I'm writing that now.
WOMAN:	Great!

4

WOMAN:	There are two snails in the picture.
BOY:	Yes, I can see them! The boy's got one in a net.
WOMAN:	That's right. Colour that one green.
BOY:	That's a funny colour! OK, I'm doing that now.
WOMAN:	Well done!

5

BOY:	I think they're having a picnic for lunch.
WOMAN:	Do you? Why do you think that?
BOY:	There's a big box next to the girl. I think there's some food in it.
WOMAN:	Oh, yes, I can see it. Why don't you colour it brown?
BOY:	How about pink?
WOMAN:	That's a nice colour ... What a great picture!
BOY:	Thanks! I like it, too.

Now listen to Part 5 again.

[The recording is repeated.]

That is the end of the Movers Listening Test.

Reading and Writing

Part 1 (5 marks)

1 a shoulder   2 a pirate   3 a doctor
4 a tooth   5 a kangaroo

Part 2 (6 marks)

1 B   2 C   3 B   4 C   5 A   6 A

Part 3 (6 marks)

1 shop   2 thirsty   3 glass   4 present
5 laughed   6 Vicky's shopping trip

Part 4 (5 marks)

1 These   2 but   3 it   4 to   5 lives

Part 5 (7 marks)

1 the/a supermarket   2 one o'clock
3 badminton   4 (four) (fruit) pies
5 (the) salad (leaves)   6 Mum   7 brilliant

Part 6 (10 marks)

Questions 1 and 2 have a maximum score of 1 mark each. Questions 3–6 have a maximum score of 2 marks each. Please see the Cambridge English: Young Learners 2018 Handbook for Teachers *for further details of how marks are awarded.*

Possible answers:

1 table tennis
2 (swimming) pool/water
3 under a chair
4 listening to music/sitting on a blanket/laughing
5 A woman/mum is eating ice cream.
6 A boy is wearing shorts.

Speaking

Part	Examiner does this:	Examiner says this:	Minimum response expected from child:	Back-up questions:
	Usher brings in and introduces candidate to examiner.			
	Candidate enters.	**Hello. My name's *Jane/ Ms Smith*.**	**Hello.**	
		How old are you, *?	*ten*	**Are you *ten*?**
1	Points to **Find the Differences** pictures.	**Look at these pictures. They look the same, but some things are different.**		
		This lake is blue, but this lake is green.		
		What other different things can you see?	Describes four other differences: • two rainbows/one rainbow • rock/no rock • big bear/small bear • bird flying/sitting	Point to other differences the candidate does not mention. Give first half of response: **Here there are two rainbows, but here …**
2	Points to **Picture Story**. Allows time to look at the pictures.	**These pictures show a story. It's called 'Fred and the tiger'. Look at the pictures first.**		
		Fred's watching a film about tigers with his dad. He's saying, 'I like their big yellow eyes!'		
		Now you tell the story. (pointing at the other pictures)	(Many variations possible)	Point at the pictures. Ask questions about the pictures.
			Fred's in bed now. He's sleeping, and dreaming about tigers.	**Where's Fred now? What's he dreaming about?**
			Now Fred's awake. He can see two big yellow eyes at his window. He's saying, 'It's a tiger! Help!'	**What can Fred see? What is he saying?**
			Dad's opening the window. The cat is coming in. Fred's laughing.	**Why is Fred laughing?**

* Remember to use the child's name throughout the test.

Part	Examiner does this:	Examiner says this:	Minimum response expected from child:	Back-up questions:
3	Shows candidate **Odd-one-out** pictures. Reveals, using separate blank card, each set of pictures.	**Now look at these four pictures.** **One is different. The book is different.** **A lemon, a pineapple and an orange are fruit. You eat them. You don't eat a book. You read it.** **Now you tell me about these pictures. Which one is different? (Why?)**	Candidate suggests a difference (any plausible difference is acceptable).	**What are these people doing?** (dancing) **And this man?** (running) **These are all …?** (food) **And this?** (drink) **These are all …?** (round) **And this?** (square)
4	Puts away all pictures.	**Now let's talk about your English lessons.** **What day do you have your English lessons?** **Where do you have your English lessons?** **Is English difficult or easy?** **Tell me about your English teacher.**	*(on) Monday* *(at) school* *(It's) easy.* *His/Her name's …* *He/She gives us a lot of homework.*	**Do you have your English lessons on Mondays?** **Do you have your English lessons at school?** **Is English easy?** **What's your English teacher's name?** **Does he/she give you a lot of homework?**
		OK, thank you, *. Goodbye.	*Goodbye.*	

* Remember to use the child's name throughout the test.

Test 3 Answers

Listening

Part 1 (5 marks)

Lines should be drawn between:

1 Daisy and the woman watching, holding lemonade
2 Peter and the boy sitting on the floor, laughing
3 Paul and the man helping a girl with her skates, near the cake
4 Lily and the girl holding the clown's hand and a balloon
5 Sam and the DJ playing music

Part 2 (5 marks)

1 23/twenty-three   2 (the) balcony   3 small
4 Monday   5 Hill (NOT Hall)

Part 3 (5 marks)

1 jacket – E (chair)
2 guitar – B (cupboard)
3 rubber – G (bookcase)
4 photo – H (clock)
5 homework – D (computer table)

Part 4 (5 marks)

1 B   2 A   3 C   4 B   5 A

Part 5 (5 marks)

1 Colour the rock on the sand near the tree – blue
2 Colour the hat of the pirate that is sleeping – green
3 Colour the cloud above the rainbow – pink
4 Write FOOD on the box with the parrot sitting on it
5 Colour the ball that the kangaroo is holding – red

TRANSCRIPT   *Hello. This is the Cambridge English Movers Listening Test.*

Part 1   *Look at Part 1. Now look at the picture. Listen and look. There is one example.*

BOY: Hello, Mrs Young! Here's a photo of my friend Vicky's roller skating party!
WOMAN: Oh that looks fun!
BOY: Yes, it was. There's Vicky. She's standing on one leg.
WOMAN: Wow! She's very good at roller skating. Who's she waving at?
BOY: Me, I think. I took the photo.

Can you see the line? This is an example. Now you listen and draw lines.

1

WOMAN: Who's that? The woman who's watching the children?
BOY: Oh, that's Vicky's mum.
WOMAN: And what's her name?
BOY: It's Daisy. She's got some lemonade for us. We all got thirsty.

2

WOMAN: I can see someone who's sitting on the floor. Look!
BOY: Yes, that's Peter. He wasn't very careful.
WOMAN: Was he OK?
BOY: Oh yes. He's laughing. See?

3

WOMAN: And who's the man near the table with the cake?
BOY: That's Paul. He's helping that girl to put on her roller skates.
WOMAN: Is he her dad?
BOY: Yes, he is.

4

BOY: Look at Lily!
WOMAN: Where?
BOY: She's holding the clown's hand. Can you see her?
WOMAN: Has she also got a balloon?
BOY: Yes, that's her!

5

BOY: And there's Sam.
WOMAN: Which one is he?
BOY: He's playing music.
WOMAN: Does he like doing that?
BOY: Yes, he loves playing music for parties.

Now listen to Part 1 again.

[The recording is repeated.]

That is the end of Part 1.

Part 2 *Listen and look. There is one example.*

GIRL: Hello, Uncle Charlie. Mom told me that you've got a new apartment!
MAN: Yes, that's right. It's opposite the river.
GIRL: Wow! Do you like living opposite the river?
MAN: Yes, I like going for walks there.

Can you see the answer? Now you listen and write.

1

GIRL: Is your apartment in a big building?
MAN: Oh yes, there are 23 floors.
GIRL: Wow. 23 floors! Do you live at the top?
MAN: Yes, I do. It's good that it's got an elevator.

2

GIRL: And what's your favourite part of your new apartment? Is it the kitchen?
MAN: No, I love to cook, but the balcony's my favourite part.
GIRL: The balcony?
MAN: Yes. I'm growing some plants there.

3

GIRL: Can people have pets in your new apartment building?
MAN: Yes, but only pets which are small and quiet. I want to get some fish.
GIRL: Fish are very quiet! And small.
MAN: Yes, they are. I like watching them.
GIRL: Me too.

4

GIRL: Mom and I want to see your new apartment. It sounds great. Can we come this week?
MAN: Yes, I'd like that. Come for dinner!
GIRL: Is Monday OK?
MAN: Monday is great.

5

GIRL: And which bus stop is best for your apartment building?
MAN: You can get off the bus at Hill Street.
GIRL: Did you say Hall Street?
MAN: No, Hill Street, H-I-L-L.
GIRL: Great! See you then!

Now listen to Part 2 again.

[The recording is repeated.]

That is the end of Part 2.

Part 3 *Listen and look. There is one example.*

Jack is helping his teacher. Where must Jack put these things?

WOMAN: That was a busy day in our classroom! Now I need to put these things in the right places. Can you help me, Jack?
BOY: Yes! I like helping.
WOMAN: Thanks. Do you see those rulers? You drew your maps with them.
BOY: Yes, I've got them.
WOMAN: Can you please put them by the window?
BOY: OK.

Can you see the letter F? Now you listen and write a letter in each box.

1

BOY: It was fun when we went outside to skip today.
WOMAN: Yes, it was. But then it rained!
BOY: Here's your jacket. It isn't wet now.
WOMAN: How about putting it on my chair?
BOY: OK.
WOMAN: Thanks.

2

WOMAN: Did you enjoy singing today?
BOY: Yes! We were very loud!
WOMAN: (laughs) We can practise again tomorrow. But now, can you put the guitar behind the door?
BOY: Is it safe there?

WOMAN: Not really. Hmm. It's safer in the cupboard. Please put it there.

3

WOMAN: You wrote a great story today!
BOY: I made lots of mistakes ...
WOMAN: That's OK!
BOY: ... and I needed a rubber. I've got it here.
WOMAN: Put it on my desk, please. No, sorry, it can go on top of the bookcase.

4

WOMAN: Do you like the photo of our class?
BOY: Yes, you took it when school started this year.
WOMAN: Some children saw it today, but some didn't.
BOY: I think everyone would like to see it.
WOMAN: Me too. Can you put it over there, under the clock, please?
BOY: Yes.

5

BOY: Look, here's our homework!
WOMAN: Oh dear! I meant to give it back to everyone today. I must do that tomorrow.
BOY: Where would you like it now?
WOMAN: Hmm. Can you think of a good place?
BOY: How about the computer table?
WOMAN: Yes! Thank you, Jack.

Now listen to Part 3 again.

[The recording is repeated.]

That is the end of Part 3.

Part 4   *Look at the pictures. Listen and look. There is one example.*

What did Anna do at the farm?

WOMAN: What did you do at the farm, Anna? Did you feed the horse some carrots?
GIRL: My cousin did that. I went for a ride around all the fields.
WOMAN: And what about Grandpa?
GIRL: He washed the horse. It loved that.

Can you see the tick? Now you listen and tick the box.

1 Who is on Grace's poster?

GIRL: I bought a poster of my favourite film star!
BOY: Did you, Grace? Do you mean the film star with the curly hair?
GIRL: No. My favourite star has straight hair. And it's very short.
BOY: Oh yes. I know the person that you mean.

2 What can Aunt Lucy have in her tea?

BOY: Aunt Lucy, can I make a cup of tea for you?
WOMAN: Yes, please! Can I have some lemon in it?

BOY: Sorry, we haven't got any. And we haven't got milk.
WOMAN: OK. Do you have sugar?
BOY: Yes, we do. And we have biscuits, too.
WOMAN: Great.

3 What is Sally doing now?

WOMAN: Sally, what are you doing now? Are you playing a game on your tablet?
GIRL: No. I'm reading a comic book.
WOMAN: Is there a film that you'd like to see at the cinema?
GIRL: Not today, but can we go another day?
WOMAN: Yes, cool.

4 What must Fred take to the picnic?

BOY: Dad, where's our picnic blanket?
MAN: I don't know, Fred. Why?
BOY: It's for the class picnic. It's OK. Ben has got one. I can sit on that.
MAN: And have you got to take any food to the picnic?
BOY: Yes, some sandwiches, and the teacher's got some apples from her garden for us.

5 Which is Clare's favourite day of the week?

WOMAN: I love Wednesdays! It's the day when I go swimming.
GIRL: I like them too, but they're not my favourite. And I don't like Tuesdays.
WOMAN: Which is your favourite day of the week, Clare?
GIRL: I like Fridays best.

Now listen to Part 4 again.

[The recording is repeated.]

That is the end of Part 4.

Part 5   *Look at the picture. Listen and look. There is one example.*

GIRL: I like colouring pictures.
MAN: Well, here's one of a beach. Would you like to colour something?
GIRL: Yes. I like the dolphin. It's jumping in the water!
MAN: That's right. Colour it yellow.
GIRL: (laughs) That's a funny colour, but OK!

Can you see the yellow dolphin? This is an example. Now you listen and colour and write.

1

GIRL: What can I colour now?
MAN: How about the rock?
GIRL: Yes! It's near the coconut tree.
MAN: Good. Colour it blue.
GIRL: OK. I like that colour.
MAN: Me too.

2

MAN:	Right! Can you see a pirate?
GIRL:	Which one?
MAN:	The one who's asleep.
GIRL:	Yes! I want to colour his hat.
MAN:	Would you like to make it green?
GIRL:	OK.

3

GIRL:	It's sunny!
MAN:	It is, but there are some clouds too. Can you colour one of them?
GIRL:	OK. The smaller one?
MAN:	No, the one that's above the rainbow. Colour that one, please.
GIRL:	Can I do it pink?
MAN:	Yes.

4

GIRL:	And now can I do some writing?
MAN:	Yes. Do you see the boxes?
GIRL:	Yes, I do.
MAN:	A parrot's sitting on one of them. Can you write the word FOOD on that one?
GIRL:	OK, I can do that now.

5

MAN:	Would you like to colour a ball?
GIRL:	The one that the dolphin's playing with?
MAN:	No, the one which the kangaroo's holding.
GIRL:	OK, can I colour it red?
MAN:	Good idea! This looks brilliant!

Now listen to Part 5 again.

[The recording is repeated.]

That is the end of the Movers Listening Test.

Reading and Writing

Part 1 (5 marks)
1 a lake   2 a plate   3 a library
4 a cup   5 a star

Part 2 (6 marks)
1 C   2 A   3 C   4 B   5 A   6 C

Part 3 (6 marks)
1 cold   2 afraid   3 field   4 vegetables
5 hungry   6 A naughty animal

Part 4 (5 marks)
1 largest   2 because   3 which
4 Many   5 fly

Part 5 (7 marks)
1 (very big) present   2 bike
3 (his favourite) (chocolate) pancakes   4 go shopping
5 (best) friend   6 (very) surprised   7 fantastic

Part 6 (10 marks)

Questions 1 and 2 have a maximum score of 1 mark each. Questions 3–6 have a maximum score of 2 marks each. Please see the Cambridge English: Young Learners 2018 Handbook for Teachers *for further details of how marks are awarded.*

Possible answers:
1 laughing/skipping/jumping
2 clouds
3 a (brown) bird/chicken
4 a (grey/green) bag/handbag
5 There is a rainbow.
6 There are two children on the bus.

Speaking

Part	Examiner does this:	Examiner says this:	Minimum response expected from child:	Back-up questions:
	Usher brings in and introduces candidate to examiner.			
	Candidate enters.	**Hello. My name's *Jane/ Ms Smith*.** **How old are you, *?**	**Hello.** *ten*	**Are you *ten*?**
1	Points to **Find the Differences** pictures.	**Look at these pictures. They look the same, but some things are different.** **Here there are glasses, but here there are cups.** **What other different things can you see?**	Describes four other differences: • curly/straight hair • comic/fan • rainbow/no rainbow • blue/red sweater	Point to other differences the candidate does not mention. Give first half of response: **Here the woman has curly hair, but here …**
2	Points to **Picture Story**. Allows time to look at the pictures.	**These pictures show a story. It's called 'Who washed the car?' Look at the pictures first.** **It's a sunny day. Zoe and Charlie are playing ball. Grandpa is washing his car because it's dirty.** **Now you tell the story.** (pointing at the other pictures)	(Many variations possible) *Grandpa is hot and tired. The children are looking at him.* *Grandpa is sleeping now. The children are washing his car.* *Now Grandpa is awake. His car is very clean. He's surprised.*	Point at the pictures. Ask questions about the pictures. **Who is tired?** **What's Grandpa doing? What are the children doing?** **Why is Grandpa surprised?**

* Remember to use the child's name throughout the test.

Part	Examiner does this:	Examiner says this:	Minimum response expected from child:	Back-up questions:
3	Shows candidate **Odd-one-out** pictures. Reveals, using separate blank card, each set of pictures.	**Now look at these four pictures.** **One is different. The book is different.** **A lemon, a pineapple and an orange are fruit. You eat them. You don't eat a book. You read it.** **Now you tell me about these pictures. Which one is different? (Why?)**	Candidate suggests a difference (any plausible difference is acceptable).	**What colour are these?** (red) **And this?** (yellow) **Where are these people going?** (upstairs) **And this woman?** (downstairs) **What are these people doing?** (listening) **And this girl?** (singing)
4	Puts away all pictures.	**Now let's talk about holidays.** **Where do you like going in the holidays?** **What do you like doing in the holidays?** **Who do you play with in the holidays?** **Tell me about the things you like doing in the holidays.**	*(to the) beach* *swimming* *my friends* *I like going to see my grandparents.* *I like going to the cinema.*	**Do you like going to the beach?** **Do you like swimming?** **Do you play with your friends?** **Do you like going to see your grandparents?** **Do you like going to the cinema?**
		OK, thank you, *. Goodbye.	Goodbye.	

* Remember to use the child's name throughout the test.

Starters *and* Movers *Vocabulary List*

For ease of reference, vocabulary is arranged in semantic groups or themes. Some words appear under more than one heading.

In addition to the thematic groups, vocabulary is also categorised by grammatical groups. 'Nouns' and 'Verbs' contain items that were *not* covered in the thematic lists. The other grammatical lists contain all relevant items.

Thematic vocabulary list

	Starters		Movers	
Animals	animal	hippo	bat	panda
	bear	horse	cage	parrot
	bee	jellyfish	dolphin	penguin
	bird	lizard	fly	puppy
	cat	monkey	jungle	rabbit
	chicken	mouse/mice	kangaroo	shark
	cow	pet	kitten	snail
	crocodile	polar bear	lion	whale
	dog	sheep (s + pl)		
	donkey	snake		
	duck	spider		
	elephant	tail		
	fish (s + pl)	tiger		
	frog	zebra		
	giraffe	zoo		
	goat			
The body & the face	arm	hand	back	neck
	body	head	beard	shoulder
	ear	leg	blond(e)	stomach
	eye	mouth	curly	straight
	face	nose	fair	thin
	foot/feet	smile	fat	tooth/teeth
	hair		moustache	
Clothes	bag	shirt	coat	sweater
	baseball cap	shoe	helmet	swimsuit
	boots	shorts	scarf	
	clothes	skirt		
	dress	sock		
	glasses	trousers		
	handbag	T-shirt		
	hat	watch		
	jacket	wear		
	jeans			
Colours	black	orange		
	blue	pink		
	brown	purple		
	colour (US color)	red		
	gray (UK grey)	white		
	green	yellow		
	grey (US gray)			

	Starters		Movers	
Family & friends	baby	grandmother	aunt	grown-up
	boy	grandpa	daughter	parent
	brother	kids	granddaughter	son
	child/children	live	grandparent	uncle
	classmate	man/men	grandson	
	cousin	mother		
	dad	mum		
	family	old		
	father	person/people		
	friend	sister		
	girl	woman/women		
	grandfather	young		
	grandma			
Food & drink	apple	juice	bottle	pasta
	banana	kiwi	bowl	picnic
	bean	lemon	cheese	plate
	bread	lemonade	coffee	salad
	breakfast	lime	cup	sandwich
	burger	lunch	glass	sauce
	cake	mango	hungry	soup
	candy (UK sweet(s))	meat	milkshake	tea
	carrot	meatballs	noodles	thirsty
	chicken	milk	pancake	vegetable
	chips (US fries)	onion		
	chocolate	orange		
	coconut	pea		
	dinner	pear		
	drink	pie		
	eat	pineapple		
	egg	potato		
	fish	rice		
	food	sausage		
	fries (UK chips)	sweet(s) (US candy)		
	fruit	tomato		
	grape	water		
	ice cream	watermelon		
Health			cold	hurt
			cough	ill
			cry	matter (what's the matter?)
			dentist	
			doctor	nurse
			earache	sick
			fall	stomach-ache
			fine	temperature
			headache	tired
			hospital	toothache

	Starters		Movers	
The home	apartment (UK flat)	house	address	message
	armchair	kitchen	balcony	roof
	bath	lamp	basement	seat
	bathroom	living room	blanket	shower
	bed	mat	downstairs	stair(s)
	bedroom	mirror	dream	toothbrush
	bookcase	phone	elevator (UK lift)	toothpaste
	box	picture	floor (e.g. ground,	towel
	camera	radio	1st, etc.)	upstairs
	chair	room	internet	wash
	clock	rug	lift (US elevator)	
	computer	sleep		
	cupboard	sofa		
	desk	table		
	dining room	television/TV		
	doll	toy		
	door	tree		
	flat (US apartment)	TV/television		
	flower	wall		
	garden	watch		
	hall	window		
	home			
IT	tablet		app	laptop
			e-book	
Materials	paper			
Names	Alex	Kim	Charlie	Lily
	Alice	Lucy	Clare	Mary
	Ann/Anna	Mark	Daisy	Paul
	Ben	Matt	Fred	Peter
	Bill	May	Jack	Sally
	Dan	Nick	Jane	Vicky
	Eva	Pat	Jim	Zoe
	Grace	Sam	Julia	
	Hugo	Sue		
	Jill	Tom		
Numbers	1–20		21–100	hundred
			1st–20th	pair

	Starters		Movers	
Places & directions	behind	park	above	market
	between	playground	below	near
	bookshop	shop (US store)	building	opposite
	cinema	store (UK shop)	bus station	place
	end (n)	street	bus stop	road
	here	there	café	shopping centre
	in	under	car park	(US center)
	in front of	zoo	centre (US center)	sports centre
	next to		circle	(US center)
	on		circus	square
			city/town centre	station
			(US center)	straight
			farm	supermarket
			funfair	swimming pool
			hospital	town/city centre
			library	(US center)
			map	
School	alphabet	music	break	teach
	answer	number	homework	text
	ask	open	internet	website
	board	page	mistake	
	book	painting (n)		
	bookcase	paper		
	class	part		
	classroom	pen		
	close	pencil		
	colour (US color)	picture		
	computer	playground		
	correct	poster		
	crayons	question		
	cross	read		
	cupboard	right (as in correct)		
	desk	rubber (US eraser)		
	door	ruler		
	draw	school		
	English	sentence		
	eraser (UK rubber)	sit		
	example	spell		
	find	stand		
	floor	story		
	keyboard (computer)	teacher		
	know	tell		
	learn	tick		
	lesson	understand		
	letter (as in alphabet)	wall		
	line	window		
	listen	word		
	look	write		
	mouse (computer)			

	Starters		Movers	
Sports & leisure	badminton	listen	band (music)	party
	ball	music	CD	player
	baseball	photo	cinema	pool
	basketball	piano	comic	practice
	bat (as sports equipment)	picture	comic book	present
	beach	play	dance (n + v)	ride (n)
	bike	radio	drive (n)	roller skates
	boat	read	DVD	roller skating
	book	ride (v)	email	sail
	bounce	run	film (US movie)	score (v)
	camera	sing	fish	skate
	catch (e.g. a ball)	skateboard	go shopping	skip
	doll	skateboarding	goal	sports centre (US center)
	draw	soccer (UK football)	holiday	swim (n)
	drawing	song	hop	swimming pool
	drive (v)	sport	ice skates	text
	enjoy	story	ice skating	towel
	favourite (US favorite)	swim (v)	kick (n)	video
	fishing	table tennis	movie (UK film)	walk (n)
	fly	take a photo/picture	net	
	football (US soccer)	television/TV		
	game	tennis		
	guitar	tennis racket		
	hit	throw		
	hobby	toy		
	hockey	TV/television		
	jump	walk (v)		
	kick (v)	watch		
	kite			
Time	afternoon	morning	after (prep)	**Days of the week:**
	birthday	night	always	Monday
	clock	today	before (prep)	Tuesday
	day	watch	every	Wednesday
	evening	year	never	Thursday
	in		o'clock	Friday
			sometimes	Saturday
			week	Sunday
			weekend	
			yesterday	
Toys	alien	helicopter	model	
	ball	lorry (US truck)		
	balloon	monster		
	baseball	motorbike		
	basketball	plane		
	bike	robot		
	board game	soccer (UK football)		
	boat	teddy (bear)		
	car	toy		
	doll	train		
	football (US soccer)	truck (UK lorry)		
	game			

	Starters		Movers	
Transport	bike	motorbike	bus station	station
	boat	plane	bus stop	ticket
	bus	ride (v)	drive (n)	tractor
	car	run	driver	trip
	drive (v)	ship	ride (n)	
	fly	swim		
	go	train		
	helicopter	truck (UK lorry)		
	lorry (US truck)			
Weather	sun		cloud	snow
			cloudy	sunny
			ice	weather
			rain	wind
			rainbow	windy
			sky	
Work	teacher		circus	film (US movie) star
			clown	hospital
			cook	nurse
			dentist	pirate
			doctor	pop star
			driver	work
			farmer	
The world around us	beach	street	building	mountain
	sand	sun	city	plant
	sea	tree	country	river
	shell	water	countryside	road
			field	rock
			forest	sky
			grass	star
			ground	town
			island	village
			jungle	waterfall
			lake	wave
			leaf/leaves	world
			moon	

Grammatical vocabulary list

	Starters		Movers	
Nouns	favourite (US favorite)	paint	age	machine
	fun	thing	bottom	noise
	name	try	difference	outside
			idea	shape
			inside	shopping
			kind	top
			laugh	treasure
Verbs – regular	add	pick up	call	laugh
	clap	point	carry	look for
	clean	show	change	move
	complete	start	climb	need
	count	stop	dress up	practise
	like	talk	drop	shop
	look at	try	dry	shout
	love	want	fix	travel
	paint	wave	help	wait
			invite	water
Verbs – irregular	be	have	be called	hide
	can	have got	bring	lose
	choose	hold	build	mean
	come	let's	buy	must
	do	make	catch (e.g. a bus)	put on
	get	put	feed	send
	give	say	get dressed	take
	go to bed	see	get off	take off (i.e. get
	go to sleep	would like	get on	undressed)
			get undressed	teach
			get up	think
			grow	wake (up)
			have (got) to	
Exclamations	bye	hello	Brilliant!	
	Cool!	Hi!	fine	
	don't worry	Hooray!	Come on!	
	Fantastic!	oh dear		
	goodbye	See you!		
	Great!	Wow!		
Adjectives	angry	dirty	afraid	boring
	beautiful	double	all	bottom
	big	English	all right	brave
	black	fantastic	asleep	brilliant
	blue	favourite (US favorite)	awake	busy
	brown	fun	back	careful
	clean	funny	bad	clever
	closed	good	best	cloudy
	cool	gray (UK grey)	better	cold
	correct	great	blond(e)	curly

	Starters		**Movers**	
Adjectives (Continued)	green	pink	dangerous	safe
	grey (US gray)	purple	different	second
	happy	red	difficult	sick
	her	right (as in correct)	dry	slow
	his	sad	easy	square
	its	scary	exciting	straight
	long	short	fair	strong
	my	silly	famous	sunny
	new	small	fat	surprised
	nice	sorry	fine	sweet
	OK	their	first	tall
	old	ugly	frightened	terrible
	open	white	hot	thin
	orange	yellow	huge	third
	our	young	hungry	thirsty
	paper	your	ill	tired
			last	weak
			little	well
			loud	wet
			naughty	windy
			pretty	worse
			quick	worst
			round	wrong
Determiners	a/an	some	all	every
	a lot of	that	another	more
	lots of	the	any	most
	many	these	both	
	no	this		
	one	those		
Adverbs	a lot	now	all	off
	again	really	all right	often
	here	there	always	on
	home	today	back	only
	lots	too	badly	out
	no	very	best	outside
	not	yes	better	quickly
			carefully	quietly
			down	round
			downstairs	second
			first	slowly
			how	sometimes
			how much	then
			how often	third
			inside	top
			last	up
			loudly	upstairs
			more	well
			most	when
			near	worse
			never	worst
			o'clock	yesterday

	Starters		Movers	
Prepositions	about	like	above	into
	at (prep of place)	next to	after	near
	behind	of	along	off
	between	on	around	on
	for	to	at (prep of time)	opposite
	from	under	before	out of
	in (prep of time)	with	below	outside
	in front of		by	round
			down	than
			inside	up
Conjunctions	and		because	
	but		than	
	or		when	
Pronouns	a lot	ours	all	nothing
	he	she	another	someone
	her	that	any	something
	hers	theirs	both	where
	him	them	everyone	which
	his	these	everything	who
	I	they	more	
	it	this	most	
	its	those		
	lots	us		
	me	we		
	mine	you		
	one	yours		
Modals	can		could (as in past of can for ability)	shall
			must	would
Question words	how	where	how much	when
	how many	which	how often	why
	how old	who		
	pardon	whose		
	what			